PASSING THE STORY DOWN THE LINE

PASSING THE STORY DOWN THE LINE

ROBERT ETTY

Rob Etty
26/8/17

Shoestring Press

Printed by imprintdigital
Upton Pyne, Exeter
www.digital.imprint.co.uk

Typesetting and cover design by narrator
www.narrator.me.uk
info@narrator.me.uk
033 022 300 39

Published by Shoestring Press
19 Devonshire Avenue, Beeston, Nottingham, NG9 1BS
(0115) 925 1827
www.shoestringpress.co.uk

First published 2017
© Copyright: Robert Etty

The moral right of the author has been asserted.

ISBN 978-1-910323-79-3

ACKNOWLEDGEMENTS

Acknowledgements are due to the editors of the following publications, in which these poems (or earlier versions of them) first appeared:

The Bow-Wow Shop
Brittle Star
Dream Catcher
The Fenland Reed
The Frogmore Papers
The High Window
Ink, Sweat & Tears
The Interpreter's House
London Grip
New Walk
The North
Obsessed With Pipework
Poetry Salzburg Review
The Reader
South

'Bindweed on the Skegness Road' was first published in *Something Happens, Sometimes Here: Contemporary Lincolnshire Poetry* (Five Leaves Press, 2015).

'There's a Story Going On' owes its narrative detail to 'Night Run to the West' by H. E. Bates (Michael Joseph, 1957).

CONTENTS

1

A WINTER ECLIPSE IN THE CO-OP CAR PARK

Morning's been too cold to face the day
and dawn hasn't really looked like rising,
but suddenly light spills over the hoarding
onto cars huddling together for warmth
and sprays all the windscreens and mirrors in gold.
A sun seems to shine out from everyone
on the gleaming paths to the ticket machines
and, even squinting, I recognise none
of the haloed, semi-translucent shoppers.
When the right size of slowing bus blocks out
the real sun, an angel I'd spotted hovering ahead
turns out to be only Alan Alcock,
who's no more unearthly than average,
but whose radiant hair and breath have been putting
a different complexion on matters.
They do it again when the bus pulls away
and the essence of Alan re-emerges,
if not as ineffably. 'All right?'
he asks me, demystified now, yet still
not quite as he used to be.

Then shopping happens because shopping must,
and we who've been bathed in unusual light
have turned our thoughts to potatoes and suchlike.
Morning wears on, and we stagger through lunchtime.
The Co-op car park's gritting its teeth
for the emptiness and a widespread frost.

RETFORD

'Fact is,' the man with a flask is informing
the man without a flask outside the tannery,
'in places like Retford you live and learn.'
'You do, Mick, you do,' his listener confirms,
removing all shreds of doubt for the moment
and giving Mick pause to sip and ponder.

To those of us passing, they're soon out
of earshot, as they were when Mick began
his preamble. Ambling past might enrich
any morning more than, for instance, *Thought
for the Day*, or half an hour with a novel
the blurb says unseats our convictions,

but hasn't so far. We could amble this way
tomorrow, though, and catch Mick texting,
or chewing a sandwich, or maybe not catch him
at all. It isn't in seeking Mick that we find him,
and what's true for Mick's not true for me,
as I've noted on outings to Bassetlaw.

But my mother was there on holiday
when her cousin drowned at Retford Town Lock
on the Chesterfield Canal as he walked home
from buying sweets. A man on a coal lorry
spotted his hair. Even if Mick meant something
else, the story would probably strike a chord.

LONDON

London's a place Raymond's never been. He says,
'What the hell should I do if I went?' He once
set out in the van for St Neots, but decided
in Sleaford he'd save the petrol.
He ticks off his shopping in town on Fridays,
and what he doesn't tick can wait.

I say, 'You know the path to Megram Farm?
Down the hedge to the opening they've blocked
with a harrow? Past the pheasant cover
and up that rough verge? There's a row
of trees on the ditch at the end,
by the gate with *No Trespassing* on it.'

We're both ignoring Sheba dropping
her rubber bone at our feet. It's raining
quite fast and the back door's tied open,
but Raymond's two miles up the path I'm describing,
watching the puddles fill. 'You with me?'
I ask. 'Right, now then: what's that first – ?'

'Hornbeam,' he's saying, before I've finished.
'Then four biggish ash, some deep pink dog roses,
an old wild apple the wasps nest under,
then sycamores, with hundreds of rooks.
Years I worked up there, ploughing and drilling.
So much going on round me I couldn't keep pace.'

JOHNNY CASH IN WEST MARSH, GRIMSBY

Somebody's playing Johnny Cash too loud
and too early for Sunday morning.
First he sounds to be up on the rooftops
and then he's growling to us down here, falling
into his burning ring of fire and going down,
down, down as the flames go higher.
If anyone didn't know, they know now,
especially so when he sings it again
as dark, handsome Mike appears outside NatWest.
It's not hard to tell Mike's a firm believer
in love being a burning thing. Spring's bursting out,
but not in his world. Mike wears his past
like a battered rucksack and takes it to bed with him.
He lives in two rooms in Beauregard Place.
Shauna Smith left her old man for him, but Mike
and two rooms were a person too many.
He's suffered as Johnny Cash has suffered –
from a fire that went wild and burns, etc –
but it isn't something he sings about.

Daffodils in blue tubs nod welcomes, but Mike
breezes past them, acknowledging me.
'Hear that?' he says. 'Now he's walking the line.
I thought he was dead, not up the Dock Tower!
D'you fancy some coffee?' We go to the nearest
café that's open. I pay for two lattes (lukewarm
and thin) and we sit at a table outside.
Mike's heard enough of Johnny Cash and calls,
'Play some Cliff Richard!' into the street,
and a dog high-tails it in case someone does.
He pours out some more of this heart of his
before he and I walk our separate lines.
A clattering TransPennine Express crosses mine
and heads where the sad songs of all ticket-holders

will drift far away on a lonesome wind.
Handsome doesn't equal happy, and don't
underestimate morning's first song.
Summer Holiday with his marmalade
might be precisely the tonic Mike needs,
at least for a week or two.

STARTING AGAIN AGAIN

He's spent much of Saturday feeling no
different. It feels as if someone has sawn
through his ladder and even on tiptoes
he can't reach the shelf. Or someone he's trusted
the woes of his world with has phoned him and said,
'Your best modus operandi is – '
and talked about train fares and tennis instead.
He senses he's starting to find himself,
but finds himself where he didn't expect.
Some mornings he stands at the bathroom basin
rubbing his forehead to rid it of dreams.
What Monday might throw up is anyone's guess,
but Sunday's blocking the way already,
like one of those fold-down parking posts
you can't drive over without the key. It properly
kicked in at seven this morning, when days
he'd been rueing right through his strip wash
ganged up and blamed him for wasting their time.
'Well, balls, then!' he thinks, after thinking it through
in a cognitive style advised warmly
online. 'Don't come your ontology with me!'

A problem's not there till we make room for it
and *Be careful you don't give too much too soon*:
such is the wisdom he's clutched to his heart,
that's seen him through dozens of worse weeks
than this. It flashes to mind as he trails
round his brown kitchen pondering on what
his next move ought to be. The answer boils down
to doing something and then doing something else.
He heats up an optimistic fruit pie

and chooses a spoon from the draining board.
Being tidy's a matter of space
and time and a neat way of tackling
the day-to-day. On Sunday he'll sort out
the cutlery drawer and start a to-do list
to keep him above and ahead.

HANG-UPS, OR GRAHAM WHO WORKS IN THE DIY STORE

The Town's Most Welcoming Sales Assistant
(a landslide win in the local paper)
was feeling so miserable during a downpour
he squelched to the end of his garden path
and howled all his hang-ups into a backpack,
zipped it and clicked a lock on the zipper
and hung it on a hook in the tool shed.
Under thin moonlight they wormed out again
and deployed a headache-inflicting formation
based on the meat skewer technique.
He bore it till afternoon tea break to spite them
and then rubbed his temples in circles gently,
which unscrewed a half-headache out of each one
and he washed the whole thing down the sink.
But being amphibious and mutable
(and having learnt much in Pipes and Fittings),
they backstroked home via the drainage system
and out-welcomed Graham at his door.

Next he selected a suitable pebble
to try out the telepathic method.
He followed the guidelines for dark thought
transference and skittered his pebbleful
down the street, but telepathy (ever
one thought ahead) ground up the consignment
into the grit that showered on the mat
when he unlaced his boots. He felt-tipped
a numbered list on A4 headed
Things I Want Gone From My Head Right Now
and set fire to it on his birthday morning.
But every sheet charred into legible ash
and the breeze blew it into his eyes.
His email to all his lost contacts bounced

back, informing him (as it hadn't them)
how fine he feels, and how welcome they'd be.

Graham's in the welcoming superleague
('Welcome, you're so welcome, thanks for your custom!')
and every welcome customer envies
how very fulfilled sales-assisting makes him.
But tell them he hangs hang-ups up in the shed
or slings dark-thought-containing pebbles down streets
and they'll find somewhere else to Do It Themselves.
Either that, or they'll say, 'Yes, well, those work
for me. I'm the one who tipped Graham off, in fact.'

UPWARDS AND UPWARDS

Mavis Bream from the terrace opposite
the carpet store at the top of the hill
(with mats at the windows since it went under)
hauls her tartan shopping trolley all the way
back up from shopping too many times a week.
'I ought to have ironed this hill years ago,'
she says, as the pavement rises beneath,
'instead of hundreds of shirts. The thing
about hills is they always get steeper.
There's somebody tilts this one higher while I'm out.
I wish I could stop and have a quick chinwag,
but I'll roll back if I do.'
                       From halfway
she sees the red blossoms of fuchsias
cascading above her garden wall.
She pampers them in-between expeditions,
and drivers who've found that the Council car park's
free while the meter's out of order
are thrilled all over again when they pass.
Generations of fuchsias have welcomed her
back to the top bearing loam-based compost
and granules of sulphate of potash. They're flowers
of notably strong convictions, and feel
they'd look only a fraction as marvellous if Mavis
didn't know where to pinch them, or how
to keep botrytis at bay. The journey
downhill with a trolley containing
her purse and the threat of burdensomeness
is something Mavis takes in her slow stride,
and sometimes she wonders, dragging it back,
how others with hills in their lives are coping,
and why they choose not to move house.
Mavis concludes that for her it's flowers,

but next door plant ladders in the front garden
and drive out on Sundays to Tesco, if that's where.
(Mavis stays on the level that day,
though the hill's still inclined to test her.)

THE OVERCOATS

In thunder, poor woman,
she'd grind her false teeth and wring her hands
in the springing eternal, penitent hope
that the growl half a dozen seconds away
would spare the village and head for Binbrook
to scare out what living daylights were there,
but a banging and booming right overhead
was her Sign that the Day of Judgement had come
and there might be Fire and some Brimstone shortly.
One such heavy afternoon one August
the Good Lord dispatched a Thunderous Winged Chariot
to round up a Cross Section of the Dead
and the lamentably not Quick enough
to Get the Hell Out sharpish. At its first banging peal
she banged everything down, whipped her apron
off and scuttled into the parlour.
On a stand in the parlour the Overcoats hung
like the pared flesh of Sinners gone hence in shame
aboard a departed Winged Chariot. The Lord
couldn't see through Overcoats, so she slipped
inside one and closed it across her. He also
failed to see trembling legs and St Michael slippers
underneath, and He focused on bad men
like Mr Pomfret still picking goosegogs outside.
She stood long in the Parlour of the Overcoats
and Lo! the storm did pass over. The clock
near the Almanac said five to five and she entered
the kitchen to boil an egg and onward
to butter the soldiers. For it hadn't been
Judgement Day after all, but, if it had, what should
she Fear? She rested in gaslight till half-past ten,
watching red coals disintegrating.
And she climbed her stairs by the Beam of a Torch
and Gave Thanks on her Knees by the Bedside Table
for Blessings, Torches and Overcoats.

MRS GODFREY POURING TEA IN OLD AGE AND A COLOUR PHOTOGRAPH

Fifty-one years after afternoon tea
this photograph lays to rest any doubt
that she smiled a little in widowhood,
with a mirror behind her reflecting

sunshine invading a budgie cage.
The blazing budgie, the sideboard's gleam
and the unreflected net-curtained window
are sharing shedding light on the fact

that when I was fifteen she was eighty
and keeping under her hairnet her thin hair
and tea-making knowledge beyond understanding.
Photos conceal all the wider pictures,

in this case the trawler painting, the ladder,
newts in the larder and Newberry Fruits.
Not to mention what wasn't mentioned,
and that she still had the words.

MEANWHILE AT PILGRIM FARM

East winds are starting to flex their muscles
across these tufted pastures.
For the information of this summer's swallows,
St Peter's spire in the level distance
points out the route to Africa. Soon the verges
won't be dotted with pinkish purples
of clover and campion. Some puddles haven't
bothered to dry, since autumn comes anyway.
Down a track off the sea road is Pilgrim Farm
(but it's not the one with dutch barns bulging
with round bales up to the roof), where Karen,
Keith, Michael, Martina and Kaye milked cows
and mucked out instead of TV, were
snowed in for fortnights, ignored the school bus,
and where Mum scribbled two-sided absence notes
about flu, floodwater and other troubles.
It was after a harvest that Karen
left no word to explain why she'd filled an hour
filling her best bag with not very much
and taking a taxi whose driver she pressed into
saying he hadn't a clue.
Some summers later a postcard came
of a park in Kent with a paragraph
about visiting soon, but if they were
short of room, she'd go. But she stayed till May,
and then for summer, dealt with Dad and Mum
(there was no one else), and milked and mucked out.
She wrote about what had happened to her
to someone who tore her letter up,
but still remembers it.
The kindness of every dawn surprised her,
and so she held on, and she held on because
she'd left before, but the tasks and the costs

were ganging up. Not a taxi this time,
but a van with her furniture in the back
took her off to her next beginning.

Semaphore might be better than broadband
and half of the winters are arctic,
but Pilgrim Farm's probably still worth a shot
for an optimist with a 4x4.
When hedges and spinneys shake off their leaves
it emerges, like a video paused,
and drivers stare and then carry on,
as Karen's dad and mum must have done,
except for the carrying on.

2

A BOY UP A TREE IN A WOOD IN A BOOK

A boy once lived up a tree in a wood,
making hideaways in the elbows of boughs,
asleep with the pheasants and woken by blackbirds
and sunbeams beaming through leaves.

His story I read in a book I took home
from the splintery-floorboarded village library,
on summer nights with my sash window open.
I made sure the book was returned by its due date,

but kept out on loan the desire it gave me.
The wish to be the boy in the wood, dew steaming
off him, feeding on berries and chocolate he'd stored
and having no truck with school and behaving

passed into wanting the book in my hand
(this time noting its title and author), to leaf
through and track down the spaces at line ends
that marked me with an X.

YYUR YYUB ICURYY4ME

We sat at two sides of the fold-out table
in our tiny front room one winter Sunday,
helping the time to pass. You'd won at draughts,
I'd sketched the Lone Ranger, we'd played noughts
and crosses, hangman and Ludo, and soon
we'd be starting tea. Then you'd polish
your black shoes and mine in the curtained-off
kitchen, where the two of you murmured
and left me alone with my Wild West book.
The Sunday I'm thinking of, you wrote this
riddle on of those *Silvine* memo pads
where grown-ups wrote memos above children's heads.
'Work that out,' you smiled and, clueless at these,
I tried to make sense of it. I might have fathomed
ICUR before the shoe-brushing finished.
The rest I've a feeling you didn't explain,
YY4ME always and still.

THE LONE RANGER IN QUICKSAND

Stylishly masked and free of dust, he was
lost in the badlands (with no sign of Tonto)
somewhere quite near the rock that he circled
five or six times every episode.

Bad men or bad fortune had led him too close
to a perilous pool of quicksand. As bad luck
would have it, he somehow slid in. The sun
blazed down, no good hombres passed, and slowly,

slowly, frame by frame, the Lone Ranger sank
deeper still. The perilous quicksand rose
past his gun belt, crept up his shirt and neckerchief tip
and was inching toward his Stetson.

This must have happened in '57,
an edge-of-seat year for Westerns. My jam tart
jammed in my throat as I watched. For twenty-one
minutes I hadn't moved. He had to get out

before the News. Was even the Lone Ranger
staring at death? A lizard skittered. Two minutes
elapsed. The hearts of tribes and nations of children
powwow-drummed from armchair to armchair.

Then Silver appeared and the Lone Ranger
whirled a lasso round the horn of his saddle.
The rope pulled tight, Silver drew back, and the Masked Man
was hauled in a dignified manner

out of the quicksand just in time. It left me as limp
as if I'd been sinking up to my neckerchief with him.
The theme music played. I turned the *Off* wheel
on the brown TV, and the white dot blurred and vanished.

Hi-ho, Silver had stirred my soul, and nothing
would be as it was. The Lone Ranger saved the day
every week for guileless old-timers and under-siege
sheriffs, but he never faced quicksand again.

I seem to, though, unfairly often, and wish
I could whistle to a white horse named Silver
who'd always lend me a helping hoof. It's hard
in a world with no Masked Man and Tonto

to ride up and put an ear to the rail track
and know, kemo sabe, when trouble's due.
Meanwhile I keep trying, in the middle of it all,
to dodge bad men, bad luck, and that sinking feeling.

OFFICE WORKERS IN THE GATEWAY TO THE LAST FIELD ON COW PASTURE LANE

A Hillman or Rover would park in the damp ruts
between white bulges of hawthorn blossom
and stay for the length of a lunchtime agenda
or Personnel hands-on that got to grips
with any pressing matters. From how much
a lad biking slowly could tell (in this case
Keith Madsen, who cowboyed the milkers),
the action plan was put two heads together
and focus attention on basics.
Keith and the cows were the only spectators,
but cows don't care about human affairs,
and anyway wouldn't know August's
Ford Zephyr from September's Zodiac.
In due course, the car would shudder gently,
cough and reverse in a practised way,
and leave with an air of shared achievement
and sensitive manual choke.
Our parents didn't behave like this.
Nor did the lovers sauntering down
as if lovers had never sauntered before.
Keith was a dab hand at graphic description,
and he was fifteen and he'd told school
to stuff it, but Keith's expertise lay more
in the bull pen. We scoured Martin's book
on Growing Up that said (in an almost
uncrackable code) that real love was private
and beautiful, and Cow Pasture Lane
was quite private.

Now there's a simple explanation,
but what's simple now wasn't then. Not them
and not us, not who made the moves, not with
hindsight, nor sight at all. Two-tone finned cars

fell out of favour, Keith looked for other
cows coming home, and afterwards
the rest of us did.
The gateway to the last field's the same,
except that the hedges have been flailed back,
the wooden gate's become galvanised steel,
and a Range Rover waits there at dusk
for morning. But not except for the lives
of others, for seeing them carrying on.

SITTING NEXT TO BARBARA

We were reading on in our *Wide Range* readers.
I told Barbara Harper in her pink glasses
the smell that was always there was her.
I wished I sat with Jean Blanch. When Barbara cried
tears caught and wobbled inside her glasses
and overflowed down her cheeks. She didn't cry
when I mentioned the smell, but said, 'It's not me,'
as if it wasn't, and turned three-quarters away.

I followed a gleam down the arm of her glasses
and shared the view through the right-hand lens,
where her *Wide Range* reader ballooned and swayed,
and our classroom melted behind. After that
the rest of school happened, and Barbara watched it
all ballooning, but surely she didn't really.

RUTH IN THE LAST WEEK OF
PRIMARY SCHOOL

We disliked Ruth Godwin. That's how we were.
Cold sores, chapped cheeks, matted brown ringlets
and laceless shoes, they would be more than enough.

When our Headteacher asked her to stand up
and told us and her she was beautiful
('Make no mistake, there's God in Godwin!')

she squealed behind a tidemarked arm
and her blue eyes skated across our faces
and not meeting them was easier.

The Top Junior Class's Leavers' Day Out
was to Dingle Dell at the end of term,
and everyone thought the school paid for Ruth

and probably gave her the egg sandwiches.
The path along the valley's rim
was wet in the trees, and caused vertigo.

We padded with care in our sensible sandals,
sensibly not looking down. Mrs Wills
(Mrs Won'ts, as we called her now)

had said meet at the seats at the foot
of the high slope. Some boys were clambering
a few yards up it, but soon losing

balance and skidding back. Mrs Won'ts ticked
them off, and ticked names, but didn't tick Ruth's.
Kathleen and Ann checked the bus and the Ladies',

and most of us muttered about it. Then
Ruth's yellow gingham dress (her best and only)
appeared up high at the top of the slope,

where there wasn't even a twig to hold,
and Ruth must have seen us and tried to run down
and her running turned into rolling and bouncing.

Time either stopped still or speeded up.
Mrs Won'ts shouted, they bustled us home
and Ruth wandered in next morning as always.

At playtime she sat in the sun sipping squash
with Elastoplast on her knees and elbows.
If she stayed longer, no one minded. The last day

was passing before we were ready.
We tidied, sang hymns, didn't quite cotton on
and left with whatever we took away.

ALL-TIME FOOTBALL STORY

When Leslie Nesbitt from 4 Walmsgate Road
told us about being Sheffield Wednesday's
all-time top-scoring outside-left, I swallowed it all
as gospel truth, but my dad said Leslie
wouldn't have the skill to boot next door's
flaming cat out of our kitchen. Leslie lived
with his mum and dad, and we lived with ours,
but Leslie was forty. He watched our kickabouts
down in the cow field, but never took part,
so as not to show off. When we fixed up a match
against Real Cleethorpes, our outside-left pulled out.
Leslie was having his hair cut that morning,
so he wouldn't be free (unfortunately)
to score nine or ten for us. We'd heard about Leslie's
quick-fire sprints, but his tactics lagged well behind
and, when it turned out that the barber had flu,
he dribbled himself straight up the blind alley
that led to our changing hut, ten-fifteen, with a slap
of grease on his hair. I picture him now, a twig
on the touchline, buttoned inside his usual shirt
(Wednesday had kept his blue and white striped one),
observing the action sagaciously
and never quite moving near where the ball went.

That day we smashed all-time humiliation records.
We still hadn't lived it down at Christmas,
and the goalkeeper took up fishing instead.
A man with legs like an albino godwit
could never have been a footballer,
but I might well have gone on believing
if the barber hadn't had flu. Leslie
deserted the cow field and us, but we'd spot him
shopping now and then. He wasn't what he said
he was, and that made him something else.
What it made him my dad explained clearly,

and I wish that had blown the whistle on it,
but it left me with doubts about adults,
face values, trust, Sheffield Wednesday
and what you should say about yourself.
This poem's attempting to touch on those things,
and it's true. Quite a lot of it. Gospel.

THE TINDALLS

What a tannery was I found out later.
It might have been why the family were like that
who lived at the end of Tannery Lane
in a brown house screened by hawthorns and elders.
Three solemn sons in camouflage jackets
biked separately into the village and back,
more closely acquainted with hedges than humans.

Tindall I only ever saw removing
himself from view, while Mrs hardly appeared
at all. Time passed for them behind branches
and stenches that hung or drifted
according to season, and measured unevenly
by calls from Bedford pick-ups with faded
tarpaulins, and now and again the baker's van.

Tanning meant skinning, dehairing and curing.
The Tindalls tanned every working day,
and thought (or seemed to think) they were normal,
doing ordinary things that everyone did.
Normal was what all the families were, give
or take the odd history, preference or habit,
and reason for keeping the lid firmly on.

Our neighbours dined on bread in broth,
washed, shaved and drank at their outside taps,
threw cinders on ice, turned blind eyes and deaf ears,
and kept the sense of a sense of proportion.
All of us differed in different ways
(such as whether we skinned beasts or fed them),
each part of the most normal family we knew.

A DOG AND SOME PONDWEED

It's longer ago than much that there's been,
but sometimes it seems as recent as Monday,
a day so impatient for self-despatch
I think I heard the whistle as it went.

And there's a thought – be careful what you
whistle for: I whistle (in a manner
of whistling) for the collie cross who used to
put up half the rabbits from First Field

and over and back to Buck Beck, where he
belly-flopped in the pondweedy water.
This happens when I forget myself –
less difficult than forgetting the dog,

and less again than forgetting the people.
Which is another thing that reminds me:
be careful what you allow to remind you.
(If *allow*'s the right word, and a choice exists,

but it's something to work on in-between times.)
Pondweed speckling a dog's head's quite safe,
but even pondweed, in some watercourses,
ought to be left to its frogs and its flatness.

Pondweed, rain through leaves, bootprints in cow muck,
bindertwine round a galvanised gatepost
might not be worth mentioning, it depends,
but any memory is there for the losing.

Bring the ones you've been hanging onto
and don't forget those that hung onto you.
If the place isn't there and the beck's gone dry,
I'll wait somewhere near at hand all the same.

THE ANIMALS' VERSION OF *PLEASE DON'T LET ME BE MISUNDERSTOOD*

I could never grasp one particular word
when I listened in 1965,
and today on the radio there it was,
as clear as an elocutionist
with a Geordie-cum-mid-Atlantic accent:
If I seem edgy, I want you to know
That I never mean to take it out on you…
Whether or not my hearing's improved,
I don't need allthesonglyrics.com
or a YouTube clip in black and white
so I can lip-read Eric Burdon:
he sings *edgy, edgy, if I seem edgy.*

Maybe in the mid-sixties the word
wasn't used as it has been since,
but it's only *edge* in a certain sense.
Others, as well, pop up out of the blue,
and lines I couldn't make out back then
are syllable-perfect now: *I don't wanna sound*
complainin' / But you know there's always rain
in my heart… Perhaps it's to do with
experience, with what you're ready for.
And more lines still, not the ones in songs,
that you heard and you didn't, that you think
you'd pay fortunes to hear again.

It was on the fifth of August, the weather hot and fair,
Unto Brigg Fair I did repair, for love I was inclined

One of life's small possibilities
is that my Auntie Dot met Joseph Taylor.
It's the singing Joseph Taylor I mean:
the parish clerk, farmhand, woodman, foreman,
church clock-winder, grave-digger, *Amen*-responder,
caller on gypsies, collector of rates,
and good husband and father from Saxby All Saints
at the Lincolnshire end of the Humber Bridge.
Joseph, of course, never glimpsed the bridge,
being six feet under since 1910, and may not
have fancied Hull anyway. He sang
in the Saxby All Saints' Church choir, and Dot
(who was only a dot at the time) used to toddle
along with her dad and mum, and assured me
seventy-odd years later Oh yes, she knew
Mr Taylor of Saxby – white whiskers,
smiley and kind. Aside from the complication
of other white-whiskered, kind, smiley men,
there's her toddlerhood to take into account,
as well as the tricks memory likes to get up to.
She told me the story about Percy Grainger
recording Joseph singing 'Brigg Fair'
(the two verses he could recall, that was),
and how Delius arranged it for orchestra.
Grainger noted his first English folk songs
at North Ferriby in 1905,
so Dot was depending on hearsay for him,
unless someone salvaged a *Mercury*. And
Joseph's among graves he dug at All Saints',
while Dot's at St Clement's, those blackbirded
places where not forgetting goes quietly on.

I was up with the lark in the morning,
With my heart so full of glee – his voice
rings out from 1905 over mists

and the mud, hay waggons, hearses, harvests
and festivals, curlews crying across the long
cornfields, and anyone crying anywhere.
All things considered, I think Dot met Joseph.
He cradled her cheeks in his farmhand's hands,
and she felt worn skin and his cold Sunday cufflinks.
She said it was so, and saying suffices,
when every belief is no more than that.
Her father was Head of the school they all went to,
which might carry weight if it comes up again.

CHANCE TO TALK

Further along from our glimpse of a wood mouse
nibbling something among nettle stalks
before it trembled and scuttled away,
he touched on the thoughts that were costing him sleep:
'And then a pheasant shrieks out *Forget*,
but the travel clock, it has time on its side.'

Sunset shattered inside the hawthorns.
How like a young man's his old man's fears were.

CHELTENHAM

I knocked a mug off the edge of a shelf.
What was in it (some felt-tips and pencils,
a magnifying glass, crayons) clattered
onto a desk and bounced or rested.

The mug bounced as well, off the desk to the floor,
where it smashed into tidy petal-shapes,
except for the base and handle. Two posies
of violets on its plump sides divided

in halves, and *February*, inside the rim,
separated between the *r* and the *u*.
Since broken pottery glued back together
is one of life's medium-sized miseries,

I gathered it, binned it, reminded myself
it was only a thing, and suddenly thought
of Cheltenham. Cheltenham was where the mug
was bought, one August, from a shop near a park.

The person I bought it for is dead,
and the children who wrapped it in tissue paper
are grown up and buying mugs of their own,
and other things that are only things.

WEDDING PLANS AND A DORMOUSE

Inside a hedge on a lane in Sussex
one warming autumn afternoon
I saw what I think must have been a dormouse.
I'll go so far as to stick my neck out: a dormouse

is what it was. I stuck my neck out then as well
(that is, I stuck it *in*, on a whim),
and in a hollow behind the brown leaves
the dormouse was tightroping down a stem.

It froze, and its black eyes shone in the sunbeam
it wouldn't have thanked me for letting in.
We'd been making plans for the wedding
and planned to go back soon to make some more,

so our heads were filled with names of aunts,
vicarious routes from north to south
and excuses for not tying the knot in church.
Dormice weren't featuring in discussions

until this one somersaulted and vanished.
Then, in a kind of non sequitur,
it suddenly became as clear as crystal
that three aunts could car-share and save parking space,

so the unplanned dormouse-observing break
played its part in what weren't yet called logistics.
The wedding certificate's been safely lost,
but the marriage is viewable, should you wish.

Of the dormouse a record doesn't exist
unless, in a way no one noticed then
(which is often the way that small creatures
and certain people leave their mark),

it's the photo we didn't like very much
that happens to show at the back and sides
how the cars are parked along the fence
with none of them blocking the next one in.

AFTER YOU DIDN'T ANSWER THE PHONE

That unanswered phone has a great deal
to answer for where our particular history's
concerned. What you told me was that you'd worded
the answer, but hadn't stayed in for the call.

It's there on my list of certain events
that happened at that time to happen to us,
like a trailer being made on a limited budget
when no one's sure of the film. But the word

isn't *certain*: *uncertain*'s truer
for how I allowed the phone ten more rings
as I pictured the hall you weren't standing in,
with the coat-stand, the phone books, mail for Flat 1,

and blown leaves like mice by the skirting board.
Your explanation lacked some fine-tuning,
but that's how trust builds, and questions and answers
matter less when much has already been said.

Our blessings mixed and stood up to be counted.
It's simpler now, and more difficult.
We text when one or the other goes missing,
but that's not to say I wouldn't phone you.

SAME CITY, SAME TREE

The horse chestnut fans its leaves overhead
in the process it's still perfecting.
Conkers shine cherry brown in the gutter.
Summer takes autumn's hint to the end of the street.

I tell you I told you once I wished
people were able to choose the memories
they wanted never to lose. You say,
'Did you? I can't remember you saying.'

3

NEARLY NINE MONTHS OF SEARCHING

'It's been nearly nine months of searching,' she's saying,
the purple-fleeced woman near the roadworks,
whose labrador's muzzled (or possibly gagged,
to ensure that she's not interrupted),

'and I'm still beside myself over it.'
The man who's listening's beside her as well,
and has been for ten or twelve minutes at least,
while I've walked to the bottle bank and back.

Meanwhile a taller dog-owner's joined them,
the wind's started blowing a chunky fleece colder,
and both of the listeners are wearing expressions
appropriate to an oral history

of months of searching (that is, they appear
to be paying attention, but maybe
it's only a skill they're honing, and really
they're working out what *they* would search for

for nearly nine months, and whether they'd spell it out
here on the path with eavesdroppers dropping by).
Doubtless their quarry will change twenty times
before they question someone at home

who'll answer decisively, 'Clearly, myself –
went missing in Tesco, Christmas 2000.'
But hearts and minds and data would have it
that kindnesses shown are repaid in kind,

and the listeners are putting the theory
to test (having possibly learned the hard way)
with Mmms and Oh yesses and subtle reroutings
toward how close to lunchtime it's getting.

Pink blossom's fluttering across the road
from a cherry branch sagging with a plump pigeon
that launches itself to the top of a fence
with feathery claps and a stick it's found.

Pigeons take less than nearly nine months
to search for sticks and the right place to build.
This one flies off again to the right place
and the gap where the stick will fit in its nest.

THE DAY IT IS

Bees are bumbling among the foxgloves,
a heat haze is bending telegraph poles
and a spider putting in eight times the legwork
reminds you of white webs before a frost melts.

Or it's late afternoon on Christmas Eve
with fairy lights draining the National Grid,
and in the twinkling you suddenly picture
long grass in a sunburnt churchyard in August.

That's how it is with a day it isn't:
a day it isn't is timed to perfection,
conducts itself in the general interest
and treasures the history of how well it ends.

A day it isn't has optional weather
so you'll look back on its flawlessness.
You don't let yourself down or show yourself up.
Both of your jokes have your friends in stitches,

the tide's up, your hair's down, it's clear early on
that you're shortlisted for small happinesses.
Ideas spring up when you need them, not later,
and places are waiting for things to fall into.

The day it is doesn't work like that.
Don't hold out hopes for the day it is,
when lows can sink so low they redefine low,
mishaps mishappen to anyone

and you're never more than six feet from a meltdown
or psyching yourself up for what's on your mind.
Days it isn'ts are safer bets, but a day it is
is the one you'd repeat, with spiders in a spin

over webs, bees stumbling in pollen
and Christmas lights hanging around for the fun,
which is why you'd repeat it any day,
and what makes it the day it is.

THE TIME IN THE WORLD

Sun's beaming through between the adverts
in the window at the bank, and the queue
hasn't moved for a while. The woman
in front tells her friend she's got it. And not

only that, she's got it all. 'All the time
in the world,' she says distantly,
which must mean she's got her friend's, and the queue's.
Except that we all have only this moment.

Except that we all had only that moment,
until it went where the others did.
Next thing we don't know, we're sharing one more.
'All the time in the world,' her friend repeats.

No one queuing speaks a word
about six words people tend to let pass,
when the context passes anyway.
And if they think now's the time to, they don't.

THIS MONTH

Season of missing, of marrows and birthdays,
and braving up to cold bedrooms and worries
that some people welcome as blessed relief
and gather round to drink to. Five birthdays
already this month in this family,
and we're not at the twentieth yet.
On mine it rained, pathetically first,
but later as if it meant it. Gillian
sent me an email composed of the titles
of Beatles songs half a century old,
and five of my seven cards advocated
a go-for-it geriatric stance.

I think it was Thomas Hardy who noted
that all of us have a deathday each year,
unmarked by congratulatory cards.
It's something Hardy *would* note, that's for sure,
but which book I read it in I've forgotten,
along with the mushrooms and where my phone is.
This month's a good time to practise forgetting,
but judiciously and purposefully,
and all of that keeps slipping my mind. If there's
anything not to forget, this month
or any, it's how to forgive, forgive
then forget. A birthday can't help what it does.

All the same, I'll be putting forgetting on hold
while I try to forgive Thomas Hardy.

A POINT AT ISSUE

At Brill on the hill
The wind blows shrill,
The cook no meat can dress;
At Stow in the Wold
The wind blows cold.
I know no more than this.

At Stow on the Wold the wind blew cold
on the day of the nosebleed, and that was
in August, so how did it blow in March?
She was eight and her blood dripped into the gusts,
and we quickly ran out of tissues.
Can you run slowly out of tissues?

I didn't dither to argue the point,
but ran inside a card shop instead,
where the man at the counter reached for some Kleenex
and passed me a mansized handful.
We stemmed the flow and went in again
to buy postcards of Stow in calmer weather.

Round the mill on the hill in Brill years later
the wind's blowing very shrill this March morning.
Here's the same face, but the tissues are new,
and they're running out now on tears and not blood –
tears the wind's tearing at, on the raw backs
of whipping hair and the first of hay fever.

The distant mauve emptyingness of rain
(unless it's a closer one) suddenly
detours down Windmill Street and we think
we'll detour via the church to escape it.
In church, with the shrillness shut out, she
sneezes and dabs more tears off her nose,

not realising, in a hay-feverish way,
she's uncreasing tissues every two minutes
and hoping they've dried since two minutes ago.
Outside it's still windy, but it's a shrill
wind that blows no one in Brill any good.
The rain's easing, though. We know no more than this.

IN PART

Carmen came in on part of a story
(one thread of several the week would resolve)
and absorbed its entire part-meaning.
What else would have sent her roaming the streets
of the village she'd lived in since she was born
as if she was losing her way or her
memory?
              Beyond the last lamppost, the moon
beamed through the iron-tendrilled cemetery gates
that she'd never known to let her down,
and she clicked them apart and talked to the grass.

This is what happened, unless it's the kind
of impure fabrication that people part-
listen to and retell. Some parts rang
untrue in how Carmen recounted
her moonlit perambulation in slippers,
but affidavits are based on less.

The part of the story Carmen missed
might almost amount to part of a poem,
with road names, a tone change and heartfelt pulse,
and silvered with lunar metaphors,
addressing the Christmas when Jeffrey checked
into the weatherboarded Sussex hotel
he'd convinced himself they wouldn't think of,
into Room 2, overlooking a car park
with dot-to-dot floodlights twinkling in
at the V where the curtains didn't meet.

If Carmen had come in and heard the part
about Jeffrey booking a room for one,
she might have gone up to bed and slept,
but she part-heard a story pausing for breath,
that had its mind set on a certain ending.

The end it headed for instead began
with Carmen talking to grass, and the next thing
she knew it had led itself where no one
expected it to.
                        What happened afterward
isn't for telling, except to say
that it's only a part, and a coda might

follow, or part of one.

THERE'S A STORY GOING ON

Nobody's bothered to move the book
from the window sill where you left it.
The troublesome fortnight you couldn't escape's
been enough to make you forget what was happening,
but when you sit down to read again
you pick it up fairly quickly.
The old man who looked like dying hasn't.
He's had a whole fortnight to fall off his perch,
but here he is still, and if not really fit
(he's just past a hundred), he's propped up on cushions
in the conservatory tipping whisky back.
The wife (who's give or take sixty years younger
and not very far from the end of her tether)
is making ham sandwiches for the van man.
He needs fortifying to drive all night,
so she piles on supportive smiles and mustard.
The centenarian's always snoring well before
Coronation Street's finished, which sets the scene for some
screen-lit loving that climaxes halfway
down page 64. And there's no wonder,
with two sweltering weeks since that kiss in the porch
with their glasses on.

Books work like that, though. The people in them
talk, act, think, feel, tour Yorkshire, get mumps, have
sex, have triplets, have punctures, have broadband
exactly as if they aren't in a book,
and do the same things to the finest detail
(allowing for different interpretations)
each time you open the pages.
This means centenarian husband won't die.
He'll always be finding the whisky's preserving him.
She'll wait herself into an early grave. No, she
won't, she'll stay as she is, because the story

stops before that. And of course she exists,
and so do the men, set in Linotype Pilgrim,
reliving any sentence you turn to.
If you don't find yourself in an early grave,
or some other grave that's a part of your plot,
you might reread it in twenty years' time.
And if that's in the draft for a forthcoming chapter,
your altered hand will turn the same page
to where husband propped up on cushions is
sipping his constantly topping-up whisky
and wife is still losing her waiting game
as the van man packs up his sandwiches
and tells her seven o'clock on Wednesday.

OF MICE AND BIRDS

It's the early bird that catches the worm,
but the second mouse that gets the cheese.
(These are just human observations,
not pearls handed down by birds and fat mice,
who'd be too fixated on cheese or worms
to calculate probabilities.)

The word is that, given the choice of last meal,
first mice plump for chocolate every time,
but the second mouse getting the chocolate
doesn't have quite the same ring. Life's
a full glass of adages. So full, come
to think of it, some of them must be worth

gambling on. Fish and visitors stink
after three days. It's better to slip with foot
than tongue, and truth that shall set you free.
You need a good memory to be a liar.
Try not to be the second bird, and never
the early mouse. Not much is simpler than that.

SOME OTHER WAYS

(with acknowledgements to Gerard Manley Hopkins)

There are several more ways of distracting a dog
than tempting him with pudding. There's more
than one way to catch a rabbit, to knit a sweater,
shake a carbuncle, polish a smokescreen,
astonish a wombat, embalm a taxi,
ambush a folk song, and two ways at least
of interpreting an ambiguity.

When Angela left the village without even
jiggling a farewell finger, she wasn't actually not
saying goodbye. You lived a paddock apart anyway,
which is usually a double-edged sword.
The kestrel windhovering above the same paddock
while you hang fire over picking and choosing
is morning's minion, dapple-dawn-drawn Falcon,
a red-gold epiphany open to doubt,
and a Y of motorway-loving bird
with an eye for ultraviolet trails
and a craving to roll vole meat over its tongue.

There's more than one means of conceiving notions
and no few degrees of justification,
so really it all depends. The reason
no one's telephoned's either that no one
has anything to say or everyone you know's
taken umbrage and wasted no time
in deleting your details. There's more than
one way to read it two ways. The postcard
the postman delivered next door (has somebody
painted your house number out?) brings the news
that life's heavenly nowhere near you.
You've seen neither hide nor hair of the dog.
There's only one way to slice a trombone,
but twenty-eight ways to suck in a hook.

NOT THE THING

I couldn't wait to make a wrong choice,
so I went out to spend the morning shopping.
I bought the wrong kind of cheese, signed two wrong contracts,
chose the wrong weed killer, soap flakes and ointment

and paid for them with the wrong credit card
linked to the wrong high street bank account.
I bought a new novel I'm finding hard going
by somebody no one can get enough of,

queued in the car park behind four wrong people
who turned out not to have the right change,
and put the wrong postage on the right parcel
I'd copied the wrong address on.

I'd still get it wrong if I shopped at WrongShop
for everything I didn't need.
Then I'd come home and sit in the cold
and write the wrong line to end the wrong poem.

GOING FOR LUNCH, FOR LUNCH, FOR LUNCH

'Hope you've enjoyed it,' she smiles. 'See you soon.'
'You will,' I tell her, taking my card.
We zip up our coats on the path in the rain,
where *You will, You will, You will, You will* repeats

in my head as we walk up the hill.
Repeating repeats itself all day for me:
what someone's just said, a snatch of a song,
a snatch of a song, what someone's just said,

but I'll leave that for now, for now, for now.
I'll leave that for now, I will, I think, because
it's not quite the point. The point is that little
prediction of hers, how she worded it

as not even a hope, a wish, intention
or promise to see me soon
(see us both, in fact), and my certainty
that she will, she will, and my certainty

that she will. She didn't mean, of course
she didn't, to make a prophecy, read
the tea leaves, our palms, the embers, the omens,
haruspicate or be pregnant with doom,

and all I was meaning was that I agreed,
I was sure I'd be back for more wonderful pasta
or one of the omelettes with Brie, with Brie,
for Brie in an omelette with salad.

Words linger on and repeat themselves.
It isn't until more words interrupt
that they give you an hour or two's peace. And if
they're ominous, ominous, ominous,

that's when Fate tends to tempt you to tempt it,
that's when the Fate that you can't be bothered with
waits at the top of the stairs. We've made plans
for lunch next Monday at one. We said we would

and it's helpful to plan, and repeating
plans helps you not to forget them, but that's
not a line to repeat outside here.
That's not a line to repeat.

A HEALTHY MIND IN A HEALTHY HOUSE

Research has proved, until it disproves it,
that anyone average spends an average
one hundred and fifty-three days of living
searching for misplaced things. Surprised at the news,
and moderately average, I'm undertaking
a Searching Review. Misplacement Central
for me is the porch, which narrows it down,
but it needn't be. Nothing's been stored or tidied
thoughtfully, not in the way that makes you saner,
like two geometrically folded socks
or a drawer of rolled-up jumpers. My system
consists in misplacing something somewhere
I haven't noticed I'm standing, and placing
more things on top of it on my way
to misplace something anywhere else.
Last time I looked for the tortoiseshell fruit knife
I added a day to the world's searching average.

If ordering space is beneficial
to anything in it and to the orderer,
I'll make it the order of the day,
and by categories, not locations.
This means collecting connected things
(such as keys and split rings, creams and lotions,
plugs and cables) and gauging each item's
beauty or usefulness. Those blessed with neither,
those that are obsolete, half-there, empty,
gone hard or soft, glued, balding, past use-by dates,
broken, flattened, not working, duplicates,
unidentified, unattached, or saved
for a rainy weather forecast
I'll pile in the black bin in black bin liners.

Sooner or (probably) later you face
the sort of sort-out today's heading for,
so let's avoid dodging the issue:

- four brown paper bags of hollyhock seeds
- a chicken-shaped blue tin candle holder
- a sawn-off and sanded gatepost top
- the pink bubble blower the children left.

All the unblown bubbles.

TAKING THE SHELVES DOWN

Two tennis balls in a vase, two stopped clocks,
lots of paperbacks that used to matter,
light bulbs, CDs and a metronome
are opposite now on the floor in rows

and the shelves are clear but for dust and bits.
The slotted screws fixing the brackets don't need
much persuasion to call it a day,
and the shelves feel the weight lifted off them and stretch out

next to the skirting board. Each batten
releases its three Phillips flat heads, and parts
company with most of the paint,
where sprinklings of thrips from thundery summers

speckle the blue we've not seen since the nineties.
The plasterboard anchors are last for unscrewing,
exposing stashes of pure plaster dust.
Time to Polyfill, leave and sand.

Taking away increases what's left, and what's left
is what's been there all along, and what's there
all along, no one thinks about. Time for
the room to seize the moment and grow in front of our eyes.

HARD DRIVE

The evening the laptop went down with a virus
a few other tricky things cropped up.
The main one was finalising visits
when all the dates clashed or interfered
and people weren't answering texts and calls,
so several engagements on several calendars
needed re-engaging. A cheque hadn't come,
which was going to be awkward,
and the hole the dishwasher used to fill
yawned audibly after two quiet weeks.
Then the question that's been too painful to ask –
and certainly to record in a poem –
was sensing its moment was near.

Downloading three antiviruses
hasn't got rid of the virus yet.
I'm looking at ibuprofen.
To second-guess shit doesn't mean it won't happen.
There's a school of thought that thinks it does,
but the T-shirt that says it doesn't's closer.
The best you can do is look after your hard drive,
and when it's infected, clear it fast.
Somebody out there would love your bad day.
(That's on a T-shirt as well.)

SELF-HELP POEM, IN CASE IT'S APPROPRIATE

1
Can you believe it's ten whole months
since what was happening ten months ago?

2
You've checked, and it is, which goes to show
that much is a matter of patience.

3
So nothing's urgent. All right, some things are,
but step to one side first, stare at the grass.

4
Learn to know when to leave well alone.
Find where the slack is and cut yourself some.

5
No trough means no peak, and both wear disguises.
(Go back a moment to number 1,

6
but don't do the rounds
of circular thinking.)

7
Some poems, like some peaks and troughs, weren't meant
for now. Maybe read this one later.

IT'S CLOSE

The daffodils are in no doubt
that December's never been so warm.
The grass keeps growing, a blackbird eyes up
a nesting site for a Boxing Day start

and buds are not only filling out
but opening as well, regardless.
I say to Tommo, who stops in his van
as I'm mowing the lawn, 'It's warm today,'

and he says, 'It's close,' and then 'Close, it is,'
as if to test airing a summer word
in the winter. 'It's like pressing on you.'
And he tells me he must be going, and does.

I finish the lawn with it like pressing on me,
but later it cools and presses less.
In this life there's always Always Something.
That's why the boiler repair man's coming,

and Nathan to fix the broken door handle.
But I don't mean these. I mean closer to
(but not this exactly) a poem's last line,
where the end's never close, but it's closer.

4

THE MOTORBIKE ISSUE

A motorbike slows for a corner
near here in the mornings at ten to six.
The time and the noise it makes hardly vary.
What I can't decide, in my half-asleepness,
is which corner it's slowing for: there's the top
of the lane, the paddock corner, the z-bends

up at the track to the Grange, and it might
be any one of these where it clears its throat
and roars back up the gears. It's like trying
to spot a microlite when you're pegging out
the washing, and the sound seems to come from
above the garage, then from next door, and then

the hand shielding your eyes from the sun.
Such tricky orientational questions
(like where the bluebottle I can hear is)
have dislocating knock-on effects,
so a day that begins with gleaming promise
takes several troubling turns for the worse,

and its compass needle misses the point. Days
prepare Good Intentions lists and then forget
where they've put them. It's a process that kick-
starts at ten to six with a motorbike
silencing birds. Then they sing again, dawn calls it
a day, and traffic will leave no corner unturned.

BINDWEED ON THE SKEGNESS ROAD

Occasionally a motorbike draws alongside
on the road to Skegness on a hot summer Friday
and roars at your car's open window. Your thoughts
have been pleasing themselves for a while,
but the afternoon has other ideas.
When it screams off ahead past the caravans
you breathe out, ease down and check your mirrors.

Sometimes it isn't a motorbike that's
biding its time in your blind spot. It and you
haven't kept in touch, but haven't lost
contact either. It's something outlived,
inapplicable, on a hard drive you prised out
and smashed with a hammer. *What's passed isn't past*
is part of the point it's driving home

as it passes you, and *Don't expect, but expect
all the same.* And how sometimes events overtake
what's happening, which means that what's
happening's not quick enough to reach the end
it has in its sights, or to reach it late
and miss the finish, or even to reach it at all.
None of this has a lot to do

with the trumpets of bindweed white in the hedges,
but it might cross your mind between Partney
and Gunby, which isn't the road you intended
to take, and you might not have, but for
a motorbike and associations
you couldn't pin down, and then for wanting to
and not, both more or less side by side.

FOUR BRIDGES ROAD

There are three bridges on Four Bridges Road.
You drive between one bridge's steel parapets
as you leave the substation behind.
The second's a brick humpback half a mile on,
over a stream they've been clearing.
Soon after this you change down
for the third, a humpback again near the post box,
where bulrushes chafe in the wind. Another,
the fourth, is looked for sometimes
by drivers who think names need explanations
and couldn't rest if they left without one.

Four Bridges Road has a bridge too few –
unless, on a map no one bothered to keep,
a watercourse bridged by the road was marked *(Piped)*
and it's crossed a hundred times a day by tractors,
lost plumbers, mothers with troubles, and pheasants
indulging a death-wish. That was the other side,
this is this, and neither's been letting on.
It's one of those roads that take you the distance
under false pretences. You count three bridges
over three streams to the sign at the end
that points out you shouldn't be certain.

PASSING PLACES

You seldom drive along North End Lane
without pulling into a passing place.
Today there's a non-negotiation
with a taxi driver school-running late, who
nods to your deference at Fleet Drain bridge.
Crows flick vees at the worst of a wind
the telegraph poles have given in to
and an owl motivated by gagging owlets
materialises above Greyfleet Dyke,

but you have a road to watch.
Sludge spatters into your wheel arches
and the tractor that's dripping it keeps you
behind till it indicates toward Swallow Bank.
Two stable girls lead two racehorses each
across where you're heading for. You brake
by the burn bins (*Only £10*) and consider
the nuisance the ashes would be
as you flash an oncoming Kia the come-on.

On the B1200 you'll join two-way traffic
and pass places such as the Folly, the farm shop,
The Plough and the church that threw in the towel
as a tea shop. You'll need passing places
for passing the places on North End Lane
at half-past three, which is when you plan to come
back. It feels as if everything's passing then.
It feels that way on all these flat lanes
up to Mar Creek and out to the sea.

CLOSER APART

When mist and sun in their ancient wisdom
draw a veil over what's ahead, it isn't
easy, these midwinter days, to judge
the direction a silhouette's moving in

further along the path: it seems for a time
to be coming your way at the pace someone
might in their weatherproof clothes with a sagging
dog, but then, next minute, you see you were

wrong, that it's gradually decreasing,
becoming less like a plodding figure
and more like a stump or gateless
post. There it goes, separating

you, not slowing to shatter
two solitudes, or face
the problem the
mist hasn't

cleared,
of which
way the other
walker's walking.

IN A MILE AND THREE-QUARTERS

Two noisy redshanks.
A wren.
A kingfisher that poses five times
 for the camera I don't have.
Two herons, two avian
 waves goodbye.
Four surpliced egrets conferring in silence.
Six swans.
The tower of the church through brown oak leaves.
A cross of poppies on Sidney Wayte's grave.
The gargoyles that always put me in mind
 of *Far from the Madding Crowd.*
A Doberman Pinscher much too well trained to even
 want to sniff me.
A lover sliding her arm into his.
Sun's dazzle on the grey canal.
My shadow attentively keeping up.
What I step
 over, it doesn't.

JANUARY 14TH

Seeing the oval, oceaned moon
behind the fourth ash tree's rained-on boughs,
I've no idea where I was looking when
I walked past the first ash, the second,
the third. It's not that I'm watching
my boots in the wet crushing last year's stalks,
or lights coming on over there at Mick's barn:
it's never until
I'm passing the fourth ash (in summer,
especially, capable always of
shock at its greenness) that I think
next time I'll stare at the first.

All the first ash trees in the long hedges,
growing there unlooked at.

THE KINGS AND THE SPECTRES
(A CHURCH WALL PAINTING C1350)

As you are, so were we:
and as we are, so you will be
is how the Notes for Visitors render
what's being announced in the speech balloon
suspended between the figures. On the right
The Three Dead sidle into the scene
to ridicule The Three Living Kings,
and one unsurprisingly pasty Dead
with his thumb to his nose looks to be
on cloud nine. The nearest King's raising
his arms in shock, while the others edge
back to watch what happens, as if
this is more than they bargained for. It's more
than anyone bargains for, and yet
it's dead certain The Three Dead were dead right,
and The Living Kings doubled their number,
dead on. The notes inform us a church wall painting
was often the way our earth-grubbing forebears
grasped the concepts of death, sin and whatnot,
and of pressing on in the light of them.
Or they stared long enough to get the drift
and left by the door they came in at.

AND AT HIS COMIENG

Hic jacet Ann, John Petch's wife, who breathed last
in 1765 and was laid
underneath these molehills. *Grieve not for me*
she begged Husband dear (the stonemason
tells us), *Here must I lie till Christ appear,*
And at His Comieng I hope to have
A joyful rising from the grave.

Hope meant expect, and Ann was expecting
to rise when His certain Coming came,
but her stonemason (who's punctilious elsewhere)
spelt his misspelling with such flamboyance
that readers who notice these things might imagine
his extra vowel amounted to
a small orthographical heresy.

Perhaps illiteracy took it as read,
or the wind was so cold when they raised the stone
that the words ran together in tears.
Her stone has sunk so deep the verse meets the eye
of a post-Darwinian worm-hunting blackbird,
so that *at His Comieng*'s slowly going.
But *Comieng*'s not *Coming*, and the jury's out

on whether Anyone's Been. Stonemasons
set their thinking in stone, and incorrectness
can pass for correct, given a chance to explain itself.
A second reading's on offer still
to the saved and the Saviours who come, or come
back, and the blackbird scoots over from patient
Ann to Jane Kime (*superiour to pain*).

HOLES IN THE GROUND

Couch grass and goose grass, hemlock, cow parsley,
thistles and buttercups, nettles, rogue oats
are so tall and dense at the edges of fields
on this side of town that the easiest way through
is to step where someone or something's
gone first and left a trail.
What might have gone first would be the badgers,
who have their own reasons for careful
path-making. But badger paths lead to
badger holes (and smell of the clan, for when
there's no moon), and a badger hole means
a sprain or a fracture for ankles attached
to unwary feet.
Paths marked in March by paws and habits
are swallowed in June by tunnels of grass
connecting cavities boots seem drawn to.
Months later snow rests on bent and crushed stalks
that mesh across holes and form pitfall traps
a fox would skirt, but a walker might
tread on and fall headlong, with a smartphone
left in the glove compartment, and only
crows to watch it happen.
The wind sweeps and pushes against the trees.
Last year it brought one down. The land's exposed
and can freeze bone-hard or whip up as dust.
Rain today's slicing diagonally,
and someone sheltering inside a hood
might tug it low and not see in front.

A drunk at the wheel of a cornering
car's round somebody's corner at any time,

or a skeleton getting fed up
of the cupboard, a new strain of flu,
or ten or twelve grassed-over holes in the ground.
Even a walk in the fields is risky.
The badgers that dig the holes help out,
but not because they mean to.

BRIEF REPORT ON THE SKYLINE

If *better*'s a word for days and skylines,
there've been better skylines on better days
than these trees marking out horizons
in thumbprints, their greenness an exercise
for the memory. Brown clouds allow
silver light a glimpse of a barn and silos
and the yellow cab of a combine harvester
that's gathered all safely in. The roof
of a spireless church shows through, but only
to those who know it is. Below the nose
of the blunt-nosed wood a light's on late,
or early. There are rooks in pairs
and crows by themselves, and buzzards figure-
eighting. And spaces, and the space that fills them,
and pylons passing the story down the line.

THE AFTERNOON SUN AND A CURLEW

Back light's erasing its bill and profile.
Its glide's horizontal as far as the hedge
that it dips behind. Then out of
(and into) the blue it flaps up – no,
two of it flap up, offering two chances
to put a name to white underbodies
and curlewings and long ringtone songs.

They head off, allowing one last look,
in the way a bird might that's not already gone,
like the merlin or sparrowhawk or hobby
a short time after the curlews fly,
which darts down the side of a half-leafed wood
and disappears somewhere only it sees
and leaves at least three new uncertainties.

ON HOT AFTERNOONS LIKE THIS IN JULY

I picture the three of us walking the hedge side
to what was left of the gamekeeper's house.
Poppies were dotting the corners of wheatfields
and swifts and swallows were diving. We found
a black chimney breast in the spinney
and broken brown walls and quarry tiles.
A sink in a corner had gathered feathers
and spikes of paint-edged glass. Tom said
he'd biked here between the Wars to look at
Jack Allen's gamekeeper's larder, and follow him
under moons and branches and learn how
to try to be silent.
Fifty years after, he led us back out
up the hedge to the road to the village.
We grumbled at flies and flapped our hands
and he made no move to brush them away,
but stepped through the tall grass, his thumbs
hooked behind him.
On hot afternoons in July like this,
when the walk to the gamekeeper's house
comes to mind and I think I can smell it,
mortary and damp, that's when
the flies close in.

LEUCANTHEMUM VULGARE AND A COW IN KYYJÄRVI, CENTRAL FINLAND

(From a photograph on Wikipedia, with acknowledgements)

The photograph catches one ox-eye daisy
in sun in a meadow in Kyyjärvi
and a brown and white cow slouching up to pose,
view developments, or even (and fair enough)
grasp the nettle and sort out this name business
once and for all. Cows usually give wide
berths to ox-eye daisies, allowing
the rhizomes to take advantage, and the flowers
to take both credit and blame. But the flowers
sway guilt-free summers away as if,
if something matters, they couldn't care less.
Classification as noxious weeds
they treat as a compliment. *Invasive*
gives them a purpose in life. This morning
they blotch the field-sides in swathes, like white
blouses someone's laid out to dry.

On days when peace of mind's absent, it's tempting
to flit off to central Finland and be
unavailable, but options like that
are for people who can. Here the ox-eye daisies
dazzle through June and then wither and seed,
and lie low for autumn.
Anyone wise in growth cycles and so on
will come to learn what the cows have learned
about what to do with ox-eye daisies,
and probably tend to do the same.

WETHER IN WINTER

The wether, who had been watching, backed off.
The blind old ewe had rolled down the bank
and lay under hawthorns, wagging her legs.
We slithered to her, our boots spraying snow.
She let us clasp her ankles and start
to haul her over ridges upward, pausing
to steady her and ourselves. We rested her
on the track at the top, her eggshell eyes gazing up
toward stars and the moon and a dutch barn roof
against the indigo sky. Knuckling her backbone
inside the wool, we raised her and swung her
to face the shed the other ewes had trotted into
the long way round. 'She'll make it,' he said.
'Or she won't. Leave her to it.'

In frost at eight in the morning we found her
dead by the corrugated door.
The wether would be the one to know how
she'd crossed the ice and hock-deep mud
to where she liked to shelter.
We brushed the frost off her nose and her fleece.
Not until the driver barrowed her
over to where he'd parked his pickup
did it occur to either of us
that she wouldn't have noticed the dark.

SOME DAYS IT GOES YOUR WAY,

like today, when John Rawson's new Friesian bull
was straddling the path along the canal,
and I made a snap judgment and stepped down the bank
and stumbled through tussocks next to the water
below the sight and range of the bull,
and a gold and turquoise spark of kingfisher
slanted up from the arch of the bridge,
and it was almost the closest I've been.

TWO TAWNY OWLS I DIDN'T QUITE SEE

One purple night in a March I was finding it
hard not to want to end, I swayed a torch beam
across the boughs of an overabundant
eucalyptus. The owls in the churchyard trees
hooted on, but there where a beam might find them
they ceased to.
Suddenly where the beam wasn't shining
ends of branches shuffled and rattled
(unlike a wood pigeon's pigeonish shuffling),
and the zigzagging beam alighted
possibly on the branch the owl had launched from,
but not on its glide through the silent dark.

In a humming dusk in Gloucestershire
as I climbed along the edge of a wood
a brownness burst out of a full-leafed oak
and started to take shape a few feet above
me, but not in time to call it an owl,
to see fans of feathers and a heart face
and feel we'd acknowledged each other.

Given a reason and an interval,
something not seen becomes something seen.
I once stared a tawny owl straight in the eyes
as it paused in its swerving near Owlpen,
and caught one I had no idea was there
in the beam of a Poundland torch.

SOMETHING OF A FALLACY

For nature, heartless, witless nature,
Will neither care nor know
What stranger's feet may find the meadow
And trespass there and go
                    – A E Housman (Last Poems)

A dart of stoat, two egrets
elbowing into the air,
a kingfisher leading its blue
laser wake, and all inside

ten yards and fifteen seconds,
and inside the hour when an airliner's
coming down slowly (and quickly)
to taxi and halt in England.

It isn't as if any of them
have checked the arrivals board
at Heathrow Airport (to start with,
it's two hundred miles away),

but if they had, they couldn't
have known which passengers
in which seats in which row
I'm picturing as I walk along,

nor seen any reason to celebrate
by (almost) synchronised darting
and flying. But if thinking's wishful,
I'll think what I wish

in fifteen seconds inside ten yards,
and when planes and egrets
fly every day
because it's the nature of things.

THE REST

A note in his mother's shy hand implies
that Richard Aldwood's conception occurred
on a warm-grassed bank in an interval
in the sailboat traffic on the canal,
which had opened in May 1770,
a hundred and three years before.

A hundred and forty-odd years later
a mud-caked, yellow Case excavator's
clawing out debris and silt. It's caterpillaring
over the path that Richard's parents
(who didn't know) ambled down afterward
and shared a dry kiss until Saturday,

and where teams of navvies eased aching shoulders
when digging ceased for a while. Oilseed rape's
sprouting where cows grazed last summer.
At Aldwood Farm, a Charolais bull pokes
his head through the bars of his pen and scares off
a crow that's flown in for the pickings.

Bulls have been scaring crows in their shed
since Pete Aldwood had the red barn demolished
and stacked the bricks and tiles to one side
in a misshapen reconstruction.
As a scared crow flies, it's not very far
across to the locks with elliptical bays

(found nowhere else) that opened for barges
the workers had loaded who lived in houses
where new houses are, where Melanie Aldwood's
moved in with Gareth, who disappoints her dad
and mum, but who can't wait to hold his baby –
for which they're glad, when they let themselves.

A Gore-Texed photographer catches highlights
on ridge and furrow, and heads for what some say's
a Black Death mound (quite near Blacksmith's Lodge,
where the blacksmith sidelined in prams and bikes).
Shortly he'll drive to one of the locks,
its elliptical bays still holding back

acres of watery land, with long fields
divided by ditches and straight roads to
villages on the way to villages
people forget to visit. He'll photograph patterns
of bricks and bays, the ironwork and the wood.
Past there the rest is geography.

CLEARING A GLADE FOR NEXT YEAR'S BLUEBELLS IN A LINCOLNSHIRE WOOD IN LATE OCTOBER

Starting a bonfire's a delicate art,
and thankfully Anthony's blessed with it.
One match, some dry sticks, a *Daily Express*,
and the fire's hot enough after half an hour
to throw brambles on it, and lengths of wet log,
and whippy sycamores nipped out this morning.
Jo and Joe hack back tendrils and stalks
with a grass blade and billhook. Nick with a slasher
is more dramatic, swirling it round
his shoulders and hooting as little oak trees,
skinnily exposed, shimmy in the breeze.
Downwind of the fire it's too hot to bear.
The middle's silver with nuggets of red
and heat-crazed branches giving up the ghost:
above it green brambles blacken and sag,
hissing smoky last gasps at pitchforking Anthony.

Smoke gets in your eyes, as we know,
and several of us are watering and rubbing.
Anthony and his pitchfork step backwards.
Further on, Stanley, manly Stanley,
whose bowsaw and reputation precede him,
has tears coursing down his face to his jaw.
If he's chosen this morning to let real
tears flow, well, hell's teeth, he has plenty of reason.
The smoke's getting worse, and we haven't all
managed to keep ourselves out of the way it's blowing.
Take Faye – her mascara's losing its hold.

PLANTAIN

'Knapweed,' his answer was when I asked
the name of a brown-headed stalk I'd snapped off
in the yard, that sagged round my hand in the heat.
'That's knapweed, that is,' and I took it as true.

But typing *knapweed* into Google
brought images of bristly mauve flowers
with lazy blue skirts of raggy petals,
and clusters of violet mops in long grass.

A different Google search pinned it down
to ribwort plantain, too common to bother
identifying, except for someone
who has a reason. What had been said

hardly matters now, nor what lay behind,
and it didn't then, except there are people
you need to believe, and plantain's not knapweed,
except when it is.